Happy Fourth Anniversary
Happy Parenthood . . .
gether

THE PARENT
FROM ZERO TO TEN

*An Elementary Guide to Family
Group Behavior, Pinpointed in Terms
of a Minimum Parent-Survival Quotient*

by

ANNE CLEVELAND

Illustrated by the Author

1957

SIMON AND SCHUSTER   NEW YORK

LIBRARY OF CONGRESS CATALOG CARD NUMBER: 57–12401
MANUFACTURED IN THE UNITED STATES OF AMERICA
BY AMERICAN BOOK-STRATFORD PRESS, INC., NEW YORK, N.Y.

CONTENTS

Acknowledgments

The essential tools for this study were provided by earlier researches in the field of child development. For the concept of the Behavior Day the author and her associates are, of course, particularly indebted to the work of Dr. Arnold Gesell and his associates. The author wishes to thank Frances A. Hines, noted orthographer and parentologist, for her dynamic impetus in the initial stages. Thanks are also due to A. R. White who, with very little interest and almost no thought, contributed valuable portions of the text.

INTRODUCTION

The Science of parentology

ANTHROPOSOCIODIAPHYSIOGENETICALLY *speaking, parenthood is not, perhaps, an entirely new thing. Nevertheless, as each forward stride up the ladder of scientific progress reveals yet deeper uncharted channels upon which the mind of man has scarcely scratched the surface, we look back amazed from our hard-won pinnacle to see vast gaps in the ocean of research which supports our frail vessel of knowledge. One such gap, admittedly, is the science of* parentology; *that is, the study of the maturation of the growing parent, seen as a vital stage in the life cycle of the human organism.*

This gap seems all the more remarkable in that of recent years the parent-child relationship has been so exhaustively analyzed and interpreted. Ah, but what of the child-parent relationship? And what of the parent's own anthroposociodiaphysiogenetic transmutation in the catalysis of this relationship? We do not ask!

Yet it is in the early years of parenthood that the still unformed Self first comes face to face with the unexpectedly concrete results of that adult fulfillment toward which it has so long been urged by folk-myth and post-Freudian science. Surely, this experience deserves to take its place beside those other crucial traumatic events of youth—toilet training, to take but one well-documented example.

But parenthood is not only trauma; it is also a period of intense acculturation, *which can change the total organism beyond recognition. The study of this process is parentology. In the present*

volume we present the results of a pioneer study in this field, relying on illustrations to underline the environmental factors where words must fail. Far-reaching conclusions might be drawn from such a study, but these we shall leave to others. As pioneer parentologists, may we be permitted only the modest hope that our work has laid one more brick on the ladder of democratic progress.

GLOSSARY
of Parentological Terms

Prerequisite to any scientific inquiry is an entirely new vocabulary. Unfortunately, many of the terms required in parentology have already been pre-empted by the rival science of the Child. We shall, however, give them a more dynamic connotation here.

Acculturation: The process of learning to do what is expected in a given culture (see culture). "Pat-a-Cake and Peek-a-Boo are vivid condensations of the mechanism of acculturation." *

Culture: The sum of beliefs, traditions, taboos and tribal laws to which the individual in a society is expected to conform (see acculturation).

The Culture: The dominant individual or individuals who interpret and enforce the tribal laws; in parentology, the *child*. *Cf.* the memorable phrase of Dr. Arnold Gesell: "The Culture may now intervene with a glass of prune juice . . ." †

Culture-age level: The mental age-level imposed on a parent by the chronological age of his child. ‡

Rewarding experience: A particularly exhausting activity.

Tensional outlets: Thumb sucking, chain smoking, wet beds, dry martinis.

Verbalizations: Words.

* A. Gesell and F. L. Ilg, *Infant and Child in the Culture of Today*, New York: Harper & Bros., 1943

† Gesell and Ilg, *op. cit.*

‡ In the event of plural children, the C-A level is obtained by a simple equation: $A^c = \dfrac{C^2\, x_5}{\pi^c \sqrt{v-1}}$

PART ONE

Stages of Development
in Parental Behavior

ɪNFANCY

Iɴ ᴛʜᴇ behavior profile of the infant parent, the sex of the parent must be considered, since there is a wider sex differentiation at this time than at later stages. The usual clinical symptoms of shock will be present in both sexes at the beginning of the parental process, but the true parental changes first appear in the female. They are largely motor-sensory.

Our typical female moves somewhat erratically, her gaze is vacant, unfocused, drowsy, even in moments of anxiety or haste. When not actually engaged in satisfying the Cultural demand for alimentation (or "feeding" the infant), she prefers to spend her time at least partially immersed in water or steam. But she enjoys

also the supine posture on a big bed, where, in an occasional spurt of energy, she will indulge in feeble kicking motions. Or she may assume an awkward crouching pose with nose to ground.

A remarkable alteration will be noted in most of the sense perceptions at this time, some being extraordinarily heightened, others reduced, others strangely distorted. The acute sense of hearing of the infant parent is proverbial, but it is not so generally realized that a normal young female parent will be instantly aware of a drop in the temperature of the air of less than $\frac{1}{8}$ of one degree Fahrenheit and will respond reflexively with an adaptive leap and snatch toward the nearest knitted afghan or other infant covering. On the other hand, the sense of smell will be greatly reduced or even completely lost, as is the sense of humor. Many females attempt to compensate for the loss of the normal sense of smell by claiming a keen appreciation of imaginary perfumes, usually located in the

[4]

nape of the neck or the cranial fuzz of the newborn. Equally characteristic of this stage are the curious distortions of vision, amounting to actual hallucinations, which often attack the normal parent as she gazes at her infant's features and expressions.

Some authorities attribute these sensory phenomena to the state of constant immersion in an atmosphere supersaturated with steam, ammonia and milky gases. Others contend that abnormal sleeping habits are a contributing factor. But since the sensory changes are matched by similar phenomena in the mental sphere, they may be seen as primarily developmental in origin.

Mentally the normal female remains at all times in a trance of absorption in her single object (or "baby"). In this state she will be found to be peculiarly vulnerable to all forms of suggestion. She has no defenses against advice, whether of doctors, nurses, aunts and other female relatives, classmates, or old friends of the family. She will accept all such advice and information uncritically, but she eventually retains only those items most effective in maintaining a high level of anxiety. She will be especially attracted to the idea of *unseen* menaces, which appeal to her mystical mood—germs, neuroses and the like. These now take the place of the familiar imaginary playmates of her childhood and enter into all situations of her daily life, lending them a touch of fantasy.

The male parent, once recovered from the post-natal trauma, may for several months show few evidences of parenthood other than a slight, but increasing, irritability. Since his own sensory equipment is still in the pre-parental state, he finds much of the

[5]

female's behavior incomprehensible. It may not be until the end of the first year that the characteristic parental changes begin to appear and some degree of rapport may be established between him and the Culture. His language furnishes a reliable indication of his altered status. The male parent whose vocabulary at eleven months includes such words as "da-da," "wee-wee" and "num-num" may be said to be proceeding normally in parentalization. Words such as "itty-bitty" and "diddums" denote unusual precocity.

Many females have tried to hurry this natural development, but the attempt usually proves futile. The still undeveloped male will resort to hostile grunts or snorts and, if pressed, may develop dangerous regressive symptoms, reverting to undesirable habits of an earlier pre-parental stage.

FIFTEEN TO THIRTY MONTHS

B Y FIFTEEN MONTHS the behavior of both parents will present a striking contrast to the preceding picture. The female parent, especially, is now in a ceaseless whirl of violent motor activity. She rarely sits, stands or walks, but is always on the run: stooping, snatching, leaping, crawling, stretching herself up to the highest ledges, worming her way under the lowest chairs. Her manner and look are alert, her movements direct and without waste motion.

Eighteen-month parents appear much better orientated in their parenthood and are beginning to acquire the mental toughness to resist some Cultural demands. Theirs may also be a rich play life. A favorite pastime for both male and female is the hoarding of small household objects in inaccessible spots, preferably near the

[7]

ceiling. But an increasing drive for sociality outside the family must be frustrated by the Culture.

The following fragment of parental sociality, recorded in a contemporary multipurpose living-space during the later hours of a Sunday afternoon, illustrates a characteristic ambivalence. The scene is a multipurpose bridge table:

NORTH: Well, now—whose deal?

SOUTH: Yours, dear. I dealt for you.

NORTH: Oh. One heart. Let's try to finish this rubber before Bobby's bottle.

WEST: Is he still on demand? I thought . . . Toby! That's *not* your dump truck!

EAST: Two clubs. You heard what Mummy said!

NORTH: Jay, why don't you play with Bobby's penguin?

SOUTH: Pass.

WEST: Is it my turn? One spade.

EAST: No, Darling, you mean two spades.

WEST: Oh, do I? I think that milk's boiling.

NORTH: Oh my God! (*interval during which North and West both leave the table*)

SOUTH: You left your cards by the sterilizer, I think.

NORTH: May I review the bidding?

T⅋O AND A H⊲LF YEARS

THE PARENT of this age shows the same motor characteristics as the eighteen-monther, but a new element of aggression and hostility is often present, and there has been a dramatic speeding up of the mental toughening process previously noted. The preoccupation of the female with the alimentary processes of the Culture still persists, but she is now less concerned with intake and more with outlet. A female at this stage may be said to suffer from *peristalsis mania* or a "bathroom mentality" and her lack of restraint in conversation often causes distress to the male. Indeed, her brooding preoccupation with the eliminative function may become so intense as to strike even the female herself as abnormal. But it is, of course, only a passing developmental phase; it will be over in a year or two at most, though it may leave its mark in a general relaxation of conversational taboos sometimes observed in older women.

FO⌂R TO NINE YEARS

IN THE YEARS after three, normal parents will usually find themselves led into a position of automatic opposition to the natural
urges of the Culture. This attitude gradually breeds a suspicion of
all the Culture's actions and motivations.* The typical four-year
parent moves warily and takes nothing at face value. He or she
seems to be constantly on the alert for an ambush or trap lurking
behind the most ordinary set of circumstances. By now the parent's
sense of hearing has been sufficiently dulled to permit endurance,
over long periods, of an astonishing volume of noise. But sudden
silence sends the highly strung female parent into a panic, and
she will sit with pounding heart, straining her enfeebled senses,
until some familiar crash or bump reassures her.

The tension in interpersonal relations characteristic of this
period is aggravated, in the female parent, by a guilty awareness of
her own hostile attitudes, and a resulting morbid fear of the appearance of a neurosis in the Culture. The frequent absences of

* Well founded, in most instances.

the Culture at school or play contribute to this anxiety instead of relieving it, since they leave her more time for the reading of books on child guidance and mental health. As the Culture comes to spend still more time in the schools, the parent will seek out others of his or her age group in a frantic and usually unsuccessful quest for reassurance.

Many such conversations were recorded during the course of our study. The following, in a bar setting, is particularly characteristic of the male approach. The basic anxiety is often masked by an inflated ego-assertion:

PARENT: . . . and you know what he's gotta have now, Joe? (Yeah, I'll have the same.) I had my secretary on the line for three hours this morning trying to find the damn thing. A kid's solid-fuel three-stage ram jet motor!

JOE: You tried Ben's Hardware?

PARENT: And he's only seven. They all say he's advanced for his age . . .

JOE: Ah, he'll grow out of it.

PARENT: I mean, though . . . when *I* was a kid . . . well, for instance, what do *you* know about gamma radiation? Whattaya *do* with a kid like that, Joe?

JOE: Ah, he'll be okay. Whyn't ya let him have one of them gammas? Just wait till he starts goin' after the girls.

The female approach is more direct, and seeks practical remedies:

PARENT: . . . and now John is buying him some horrible atomic rocket thing. I'm simply terrified!

GUEST: Yes, I know. I used to think animals were the solution. We got a couple of rabbits for Timmy last Easter . . .

[11]

PARENT: I can just *see* the whole house going up in smoke!

GUEST: *We* keep them out in the yard. There are about seventeen now.

PARENT: . . . and it uses some disgusting, smelly fuel that probably explodes if you look at it. It'll be all over the rugs anyway.

GUEST: Timmy was supposed to keep them cleaned up but . . .

PARENT: Aren't there *any* safe, quiet hobbies for a seven-year-old?

GUEST: Well, you know—rabbits . . . they *are* educational . . .

TꟽN YEARS AND AFTER

As TIME goes on, the inexorable developmental drive of parent-hood begins to heal the raw edges of anxiety, bringing comparative peace of mind and even a measure of optimism. The age of ten generally sees parental optimism at its peak. This is a period of false confidence, during which parents will often congratulate themselves, and even each other, on their successful handling of past Cultural problems.

This is what gives to the age of adolescence its special shock value. Too much has already been written about the trauma of adolescent parenthood to need repetition here. Suffice it to say that the basic problem is a complete loss of self-confidence in the parent. Many factors will help to determine the character of the outward symptoms, however. The uneasy sense of failure may lead

to a pitiful attempt to placate the Culture or, in reaction, to an orgy of righteous indignation. Either sex may assume either role, or both at once. The adolescent parent will react best to a very permissive handling, but where this is not possible, the services of a specialist may be required.

PART TWO

The Behavior Day

THE FOREGOING Behavior Profiles were too brief to do more than indicate the course that a developmental study of parenthood might pursue. In order to comprehend the nature of the Cultural pressures which can produce such profound, if temporary, alterations of personality, we must turn to observation of the parent's Behavior Day. Let us now select a pair of parents in the middle culture-age level and follow them into their home, where we can study more closely their attempts to function adaptively among the stimuli and the frustrations of their daily routine in the Cultural nexus.

1.

IN A typical Behavior Day the parent awakens between 5 and 7
A.M. In almost every case parents need help to effect the difficult
release from sleep into waking and will show more or less resistance.
It is at this time that the male parent's sensitivity to Cultural impress

is greatest. Indeed, he may often acquire a sense of other Selves
before he achieves a clear sense of his own Self.

The female parent will usually show a more advanced grasp of the total situation. Nevertheless, this period of early-morning sociality, which might be expected to yield a lively exchange of ideas and information, may prove disappointing, since the parent will frequently fail to respond to intellectual stimulation.

2.

THE PERIOD immediately after arising is generally a difficult one, especially for the female parent, as she has not yet become adjusted to the upright position. Later she will dart and dash, charged with runabout compulsions, but now she lurches as she walks, clutching tables, cribs, and even the stove for physical support. Moving amid a welter of conflicting stimuli, her responses continue for some time to be groping, confused, and contradictory.

3.

IT IS interesting to note that the male parent seems to fare better at this period and will, indeed, give evidence of remarkable powers of concentration in his single-minded drive toward the morning goal. After his toilet routines comes the morning meal. If the male is on a self-demand schedule for this meal, his vigorous self-activity might strike an untrained observer as disorientated. On closer examination, however, it will be revealed as fully purposive and capable of producing a structured end product.

A structured end product.

In households where group feeding is the rule, the male is passive, but when served he will drink his coffee well and rapidly and there is some tendency to demand repetition. By now his motor-sensory apparatus is in relatively continuous focus and he is able to combine feeding with the enjoyment of simple stories based on real-life events. He does not sit long in his chair, however, and it is unusual for this meal to be completed.

He is beginning to have thoughts of a destination, and his behavior becomes increasingly ritualistic. Soon his attention will be completely withdrawn from the home situation. Certain well-trained males may signalize the moment of departure with a kiss for the female, if she is available, but for many an emphatic closing of the front door will seem sufficient.

4.

Now let us observe the behavior of the female parent during the period we have just covered. At first vague and fumbling, her actions will gradually become more purposeful. Soon they will harden into a recognizable mold—what has been called the Maternal Preschool behavior pattern.

"Is this the right way?"

"I can't wear that thing!"

Certain key phrases, in daily use by the Culture, help to effect this transition and give the parent a thrust in the right direction.

"I can't find it."

The preschool behavior pattern is characterized by ruthless determination. The parent is imperious, demanding, stubborn, as she attempts to impose her will on her environment and assert the superiority of her claims. The most legitimate demands of the Culture will receive short shrift at this time, even claims for medical attention being callously ignored. The preschool parent's preoccupation with clocks might well appear obsessive to an observer who failed to recognize the strong element of self-preservation underlying the preschool drive.

"It's no FAIR! She ate the Free Atomic Ring!"

5.

WITH the departure of the school bus, the parent gladly shifts from group to solitary interests. This is a period of emotional and physical recuperation, and what may appear to be indolence is in reality a slow climb toward the next plateau of equilibrium.

The importance of relaxation at this time cannot be overemphasized. Cases are known where a sudden interruption of this recuperative period has led to severe shock and subsequent tantrums or other undesirable behavior.

". . . just wanted to be sure you knew this is your day to drive the children to nursery school—you remember, Louise arranged it last week when I changed with Mrs. Jennings after the baby had his shots—well, her Johnny spent last night with Benny Schwartz and Ellen just called to say would you mind picking up Sally first because Billy is just starting his cereal—and you could get over to the Schwartzes' in between . . ."

6.

How suddenly the pendulum swings in our typical parent's Behavior Day! As her early morning tensions drop away, her spontaneous sense of time again makes itself felt. She is now ready for a period of active employment. Her activities run the gamut from precise manipulations, such as picking up small objects from the

floor and fingering them, to such gross motor activities as pushing and pulling heavy objects and putting large objects into smaller ones.

7.

THE PARENT may remain for some time engrossed in her runabout activities, but sooner or later she will feel the need for a broader scene. It is now time for her outing, which will usually include an expedition to the local supermarket.

Although nearly all female parents find the highly complex environment of a supermarket invigorating, many cannot be depended on for self-regulation at this time. Surrounded by an abundance of stimuli, the average parent shows a tendency to dawdle and procrastinate, and may require help from the Culture to effect a transition. One or two of the techniques illustrated will often prove effective by *activating* her in the right direction.

A. Gently leading the parent is often more successful than verbal handling.

B. A humorous approach may distract the parent from other stimuli.

C. Parents love to chase and be chased—a characteristic which may be put to positive use.

8.

THE PARENT may now spend an hour at a playground or park, where she will find many of her peers. Parents are naturally gregarious in these surroundings and the group will associate in an amicable manner so long as the underlying *parent rivalry* * is not overstimulated. At such times the Culture will do well to maintain a tactful distance and even "refuse" when called upon to demonstrate a talent or dimension.

* Parent rivalry more intense than the closest sibling rivalry invariably exists between two parents of the same culture-age level, even when they are in no way related and may even be meeting for the first time.

9.

FOR MANY parents of the appropriate culture-age level, the drive to or from a nursery school provides the occasion for an intensification of the acculturation process which may be richly rewarding. While the parent's hands are occupied with the mechanical details of driving, her mind is free to receive Cultural impress. The Culture will most often take advantage of this on the return journey. The curriculum should include art appreciation, with special reference to current artifacts, and group discussion, preferably on ethical subjects such as fair play and individual property rights.

10.

AFTER the morning's outing, the parent is ready for lunch, a light meal which may be taken in a standing position or while moving about the room. It may consist of a few spoonfuls of strained applesauce, half a peanut-butter sandwich and a sip or two of chocolate milk.

Surprisingly, although the parent will often voluntarily choose such a meal, forced feedings of the same menu have been known to result in temporary loss of appetite.

11.

AFTER LUNCH, the parent, if possible, enjoys the supine. The Culture may find leisure during this interval to indulge in various forms of self-expression.

12.

MOST parents do better if not awakened from a nap too suddenly. The Culture will find it advisable not to approach the bed or couch directly, but to busy itself quietly about the room. In time the return of the school bus will speed the waking process.

"Untie it!"

13.

REFRESHED by her nap, the parent is now ready for free play. Soon she will begin to move about the house, and it is at this time that she is most readily drawn into group activities.

The transition may be made through a verbal appeal for help from a member of the group, such as "Button it!" or "Untie it!" However, if the parent is still unwilling to participate actively, repetition of the meaningful phrases "That's MINE!" or "It's no FAIR!" will accomplish the desired result.

"It's no FAIR! She's bullet-proof!"

"You can't help <u>him</u>! He's the Bad Man!"

14.

WHEN the parent is ready for active participation, she may for a short time become vigorously involved. She is usually handicapped, however, by a very rudimentary ethical sense which makes it difficult for her to accept the rules of the game. Moreover, a mother's instinctual need to protect and to disinfect her young is often in conflict with the requirements of the group.

15.

Toward the end of the afternoon the parent will tend to return to a quiet self-activity such as reading, but not for long. A period of violent motor activity then ensues. This change comes about as the result of the female's renewed awareness of her environment. Her sensitivity to her physical surroundings seems to be momentarily heightened by anticipation of the male parent's return. Although she herself may be relaxed and at ease in the atmosphere normally provided by the Culture, she has been made aware that

the male, coming from a day spent in other, or *nonparent*, surroundings, must be helped to make the transition by a temporary
simplification of the environment.

16.

THE average male parent returns home between 6 and 7:30 P.M. He will be greeted with enthusiasm, but is soon ignored. He invariably finds this period of adjustment a difficult one. If an attempt is made to draw him into the activities of the group he will withdraw sullenly, complaining of fatigue. Nevertheless he tends to show his resentment of Cultural interests in which he is not included.

It has been found that no true communication takes place on the verbal level during this period. Verbalizations are parallel, or at most diagonal, meeting at obtuse angles.

CHORUS OF CHILDREN: Hi, Daddy! Hey Daddy! Daddy, Daddy, Daddy! Daddy's come home!
MALE PARENT: Hi.
FEMALE PARENT: Hi, Daddy.
CHORUS: Hi, Daddy! Hey, Daddy! Daddy, Daddy, Daddy! Daddy's come home!

MALE P: Did you deposit that check?

1ST CHILD: Daddy, look, I'm a cowboy who only likes to wear one boot.

2ND CHILD: I'm a rabbit. I'm the cowboy's girl friend.

1ST CHILD: Daddy, you be a horse.

MALE P: Not now, kids. I'm too tired to be a horse.

2ND CHILD: You can be a *tired* horse then.

3RD CHILD: Daddy, horse?

FEMALE P: Children, have you washed yet? Supper's almost ready.

MALE P: Did you deposit . . . ?

FEMALE P: Go and wash your hands! What, dear?

MALE P: I said, did you—

CHORUS: Stick 'em up! Bang, bang! Pow! Ping yaaa-ow!

1ST CHILD: Yipes, they got me.

2ND CHILD: Mummy's the bad man. You're dead, Mummy.

3RD CHILD: Daddy, horse?

MALE P: Out of the kitchen! Go on, all of you!

FEMALE P: Supper's almost ready. What deposit, dear?

1ST CHILD: Hey, a deposit? Gold, gold! We're rich!

2ND CHILD: Then can I buy a horse, Daddy?

FEMALE P: Children, *do* go and wash—Daddy wants to talk to Mummy.

2ND CHILD: . . . and can we have a horse's girl friend, so we can have baby horses?

MALE P: No! Out of the *kitchen*!

FEMALE P: Sorry, dear. What were you telling me?

MALE P: I wasn't telling, I was *asking*—

FEMALE P: Yes, John, I heard you. Jay, what's the matter, honey?

3RD CHILD: Daddy, horse?

A more satisfactory transition can sometimes be effected by moving the male parent's bath (or shower) to this time of day. In the bath his tensions ease and he vocalizes happily to himself, gurgling, growling and making high squealing sounds. He is happier alone at this period.

17.

AFTER HIS BATH, or other temporary retreat, the male may be more relaxed in his response to the total situation. Now he can often amuse himself for long periods by pouring liquids from one receptacle into another. His fussing at this time is primarily for social attention.

18.

THE EVENING MEAL as a group process has often been considered of particular value in parent acculturation. It is true that at such a meal the parents comprise a "captive audience." Important information may be more readily conveyed to them in this situation. Nevertheless, it is the belief of the present author that a parent, especially a male parent, does not really belong in a group situation at this time, since both motor and emotional control are frequently at a low ebb. Tantrums are not at all uncommon; at best the parent will be an inattentive listener and negative in his approach to most subjects. Even well-adapted parents will attempt to relieve their tensions through some form of undesirable behavior, such as cigarette or cigar smoking, compulsive chatter about subjects of no general relevance, or an obsessive concern with the amount and kind of food consumed by other members of the group.

In this tape recording,* made by two field workers during the evening meal at the home of Mr. and Mrs. John W., Tuesday, April 28, 1956, we observe how group discussion is frustrated by the characteristic negativism of the male parent, although the subject is of great intrinsic interest:

FIRST CHILD: Daddy, how much blood would there be if you cut a dinosaur's head off?

MALE PARENT: I've no idea, Mike. Eat your spaghetti and meat balls.

FIRST CHILD: Timmy said if you cut a dinosaur's head off, you'd have a whole swimming pool full of blood. Is that true, Daddy?

MALE P: I don't know and I'd prefer not to discuss it at the table.

FIRST CHILD: Wow! A whole swimming pool full of blood! What if you fell in?

MALE P: I said we would not discuss it any further! Eat your dinos—spaghetti!

SECOND CHILD: Mummy, do I really have to have Sandra to my party? She smells funny.

FIRST CHILD: So do you smell funny.

SECOND CHILD: I don't.

FIRST CHILD: You do.

SECOND CHILD: I don't!

FIRST CHILD: You do too.

SECOND CHILD: I don't! Mummy, *do* I smell funny?

FIRST CHILD: Oh boy, look at me eating my dinosaur! All bloody . . . (*murmuring*) Blood . . . blood . . .

FEMALE P: (*Enters with milk*) John! You're not *eating*! How can you expect the children . . .

* Soon to be available on LP QT–98305986. Folkways.

19.

IN SOME households the parents are permitted to take their evening meal alone at a much later hour. The behavior of such parents is likely to show a marked regression to pre-parental patterns—the

female may even light candles, as in the rituals of courtship. Since by such means the value of the day's acculturation may be seriously impaired, it is not really advisable to allow regressive habits of this kind to become established. Fortunately the accepted bedtime-delaying tactics can be used here with telling effect.

20.

THE pre-bed period has been called the greatest ordeal of the Behavior Day. In the female parent it inevitably produces a behavior syndrome closely resembling the preschool pattern.

Authorities in the allied field of child study have long attempted to indoctrinate parents with the importance of peace, or a truce, at bedtime. But the female seems unable to reconcile this aim with the sanitary procedures which she considers necessary for Cultural

survival. She will nevertheless try to carry out one or two of the recommended techniques of pacification, perhaps the reading aloud or the *quiet little talk*. The healthy-minded Culture will certainly reject the parent's choice of reading, however, preferring a more factual approach to subjects such as cannibalism, volcanic eruptions, disasters at sea, undersea adventures with Giant Squid or Giant Clam, or the daily diet and table manners of Tyrannosaurus Rex. We cannot help feeling that the sensitive, imaginative parent is better off without such fare. A similar hazard is encountered in the quiet bedtime chat. The parent may be so overstimulated by partial revelations of the Culture's extramural activities that the tone of the discussion rapidly deteriorates.

When it comes to the final act of release, few parents of either sex are equipped to withstand the organized Cultural resistance usually encountered at this time. There are many simple delaying tactics, such as the various water gambits, which can be counted on to render a parent temporarily docile. The Culture should be prepared for an occasional tantrum, however. When this occurs, the acting-out of the parent's repressed hostility brings a welcome release of tension and may even have a quieting effect on the situation as a whole.

21.

WITH the successful elimination of immediate Cultural pressure, the female is left to her own devices. She will often feel a need for reassurance. Together with the male she may perhaps enjoy an entertainment consisting of simple pictures with few details. As

fatigue sets in it is often difficult for her to organize her activities; for example, if too many objects are put out for her, she becomes confused. At such times it is possible to help her by handing her one familiar object at a time.

22.

As THE HOUR of sleep approaches, the parents' behavior assumes again a ritualistic character. Food is sought by the male, although he may still be replete from a heavy dinner; doors and windows must be opened and closed according to prescribed rules. The female also has purification and adornment rituals. Finally the Culture itself must be formally inspected, ritually drained, watered,

covered. By such actions as these the parents regain a sense of mastery over the environment. The actual release into sleep may then be easily effected, perhaps through an act as simple as the laying of a medium-sized book, page side down, over the upper part of the abdomen.*

And here we may leave our representative parents, poised in the precarious equilibrium of a temporarily achieved physiological well-being, to complete the wholesome developmental cycle of the Behavior Day.

* In a few stubborn cases it may be necessary to read a chapter or two of the book before applying it.

APPENDIX

Guidance in Specific Areas

In the foregoing Behavior Day we have seen how even everyday occurrences may involve sufficient stress and conflict to produce "problem" behavior in a normal parent. There are in addition a certain number of other "problem" occasions which occur frequently enough in the life of our representative culture-nexus (or "family") to merit specific guidance suggestions.

It is important for the Culture to discover *why* certain situations seem inevitably to "bring out the worst" in an otherwise docile and well-adapted parent. Problem behavior is an outward symptom of any significant increase of inner tension. In the following pages we shall attempt to indicate the nature of the underlying tensions in a few such situations and suggest how, by wise handling, they may be eased, and the worst of the concurrent symptoms forestalled.

Characteristic startle-pattern in a well-nourished male who has been inadequately prepared.

I.

AN AVERAGE PARENT, no matter how well adjusted to his own Culture, is shy with strangers. Care should always be taken to prepare him in advance for the appearance of the Culture's associates.

In this female, enthusiasm for organized sport has been allowed to reach the unmanageable stage.

Events such as the Culture-birthday will be especially trying to this type of parent, since, by the nature of the occasion, he is denied the usual resource of flight. In order to mask his underlying panic, he (or more usually she) will probably resort to a frenzy of enthusiastic "organization," and become so hyperactive that she may be difficult to control.

The most successful way for the Culture to handle this problem is *before* the event, by providing a large number of stimulating activities to occupy the parent up to the very moment when the guests are expected. Balloons should be demanded in large numbers. They will provide an hour or two of healthful exercise and may prove sufficiently exhausting so that no further measures are re-

Balloon therapy is recommended.

quired. The manufacture of elaborate decorations and refreshments should also be encouraged. The final, or "Zero" hour should be occupied by the toilette of the Culture. Girls will find a frequent change of costume and the addition of ribbons, flowers, plastic ornaments, etc., to the coiffure most effective in "fixating" a female parent. Boys will do better by refusing to dress at all. They may then capture the parent's undivided attention by brilliant sophistry in the ensuing debate.

" . . . but at Pammie's party they had hot dogs _too_, and jelly doughnuts _and_ cupcakes _and_ the ice cream was shaped like a rabbit. And Muffie's cake had _four_ different kinds of icing on it. . . ."

If, in spite of suitable preparation, the parent remains excitable, hyperactive and determined, it is best to demand the refreshments immediately. Ice cream and cake may then be tastefully combined with crêpe paper and applied in various ways to the table, the guests, and the furnishings of the room, to provide a rich play experience and an absorbing occupation for the parent's remaining leisure hours.

II.

FEAR of strange places enters into a large group of tension-situations. To list only a few, they are: expeditions to zoos, museums, circuses, theaters, beaches and ball games. It is curious to note that one or both parents may previously have made unusually successful adjustments to some of these environmental situations during the pre-parental stage. The parental process, however, with its roots deep in the primordial racial past, revives primitive fears of Nature and the Unknown. In the grip of these obscure terrors, parents fall easily into equally primitive patterns of behavior. The ancient myth of Parental Dominance may then possess them to the point where all acculturation is forgotten. The onset of this com-

Satisfactory adjustment to Nature in the pre-parental period.

plex is marked by various physical symptoms: an imperious and aggressive manner, loud voice, immoderate gestures. The veins of the head and neck may swell and the features become suffused, the eyeballs roll rapidly from side to side until they become hypnotically fixed upon some member of the Culture. The *sense of time* is abnormally heightened, and a parent in this state is obsessed with time-symbols—clocks, timetables, etc. In the early stages of the expedition, he, or more especially she, will be acutely aware of any disorder or lack of symmetry in the *appearance* of

The Station Platform Syndrome.

the Culture. Indeed, she may become so fixated on the hair, hands or nose of the Culture that the actual objective of the expedition will pass almost unnoticed.

There is, unfortunately, very little that the Culture can do to relieve the basic anxiety underlying this problem behavior. If the

Effective use of mechanical restraints.

Culture is permissive ("obedient" and inert), the parent will simply interpret this as a sign of impending illness. It *is* possible, however, to reduce the restless hyperactivity, which is so exhausting, by the use of various mechanical restraints. The well-known "Here, hold this" technique is excellent for temporary immobilization and can be used effectively in any of the abovementioned situations.

It is obvious from the foregoing that both the parents and the Culture would do better on these occasions if their spheres of action could be kept separate. But this is not always easy to achieve, since the parent tends to cling for reassurance, especially to the younger members of the group. Where the accompanying parent is of the opposite sex, the Culture may find that a trip to the "Rest Room" provides the necessary break. In a museum, the Culture should feign prolonged interest in a partially decomposed mummy in order to alienate the parent's attention from his immediate vicinity.* At the beach, a deep hole in the sand becomes a useful prop—for some reason the sight of the Culture industriously busied with spade and

* The Reptile House in the zoo may be used in the same way.

Here, almost total immobilization has been achieved by the use of only the simplest materials, which may be brought from home or purchased in any public park or zoo.

pail has a mysteriously soothing effect on parents and relaxes their vigilance at once.

It is important to remember, however, that all these techniques for bringing about a separation of Culture and parents interests are only effective in the long run if the Culture itself remains in a position to end the separation at will. If the parent must exert himself seriously in this direction, the situation can only change for the worse.

III.

PARENT RIVALRY may be the source of a serious behavior disturb-
ance which symptomatically resembles the fear-reactions previously
noted. In its worst form it is apt to occur only in mixed groups of
relatives who gather not more than three or four times a year to
celebrate their mutual existence, usually on the occasion of a
national holiday. In the guidance of such mixed groups, the Culture
will find it absolutely essential to maintain a united front with the

An excellent example of the united front.

other Culture representatives present, especially on matters of etiquette. There must be no individual "examples" of untoward excellence. Needless to say, the parents' inflated notions of status should not be pandered to by any demonstrations of prowess in athletics, memory, virtue, altitude or dental productivity.

There is only one recommended exception to the rule of modesty and detachment which is the attitude mandatory for the Culture whose parent is in the grip of acute parent rivalry. This is in the matter of food. Here gross indulgence is in order, since too much discretion is likely to focus the unwelcome attention of the whole parental group on the individual abstainer.

How fortunate it is that the intensity of the passion aroused by parent rivalry makes it also short-lived! The parent cannot remain too long in such a group situation without becoming exhausted. At this point the Culture can tactfully inquire the time of the proposed return "home" without fear of any but token resistance.

About the Author

Anne Cleveland writes:

"*My interest in psychology and allied subjects began at the age of fourteen, when I came across a book called, I think,* Problems of Male Adolescence. *I have three brothers.*

"*I went to school in Ohio, Wisconsin, France, Switzerland and Massachusetts, ending as an art major at Vassar, where I was voted "Most Absent-minded." Collaborated with Jean Anderson on* Vassar, a Second Glance *and* Everything Correlates. *Odd jobs drawing and teaching until the war and a couple of years in the WAC doing some even odder jobs.*

"*Married in 1949. Spent the first five years of marriage in Hong Kong and Japan, where I produced two children, Toby and Susan, and a book,* It's Better with Your Shoes Off.

"*I am now living the normal schizoid life of a commuter's wife in Weston, Connecticut.*"